BELIEVE

COLLECTION OF POEMS

AARNA KAPOOR

Made with ♥ on the Notion Press Platform
www.notionpress.com

For my extraordinary parents,

The architects of my courage and the keepers of my heart.

In your faith, I found my voice;

In your love, I discovered my wings.

This book is but a fragment of the gratitude I carry for you—

My constant, my forever, my home.

Contents

Contents

Foreword

What does it mean to hold the echoes of yesterday while chasing the promises of tomorrow? Can the roots of our history and the wings of our dreams coexist in harmony? In Believe, Aarna Kapoor invites us to explore these timeless questions, offering a collection of poems that intertwine reflection with self-discovery, past with present. Each verse is a bridge, drawing us closer to understanding how identity evolves—not as a fixed point, but as a journey that continually shapes who we are.

This collection is more than poetry; it is a conversation—one that flows between the traditions of the past and the innovations of the future, between self-doubt and the resilience to rise. With every poem, Aarna unpacks the complexity of identity, offering not just questions, but answers that grow richer with each line. You will find that these poems resonate deeply, not only as personal musings but as universal truths.

Aarna Kapoor's voice is both introspective and empowering. Through her words, she motivates and challenges readers to embrace their own journey of growth and self-discovery. "Believe" is a quiet revolution—one that urges us to ask hard questions, confront our own fears, and find the strength to believe in ourselves, even when the path seems unclear.

As you turn these pages, you'll encounter poems that will make you reflect on the weight of expectations, the ache of longing, and the triumph of embracing the present moment. Each piece speaks to the heart, urging you to recognize that the light of resilience shines brightest in the most uncertain times.

Believe is more than a poetry collection—it is a companion for those seeking to understand themselves, to navigate the complexities of identity, and to embrace the possibilities of tomorrow. It reminds us that we are all shaped by the echoes of our history and the dreams that drive us forward. Every journey—no matter how uncertain—is worth taking. It is with great admiration that I present this book. May these pages be as much a source of inspiration to you as they have been to me. Let the words of 'Believe' guide you, challenge you, and, above all, remind you that you are both your roots and your wings.

Vani Anand
Proof Reader

Preface

What does it mean to belong to many worlds at once? To carry the weight of history in one hand and the hope of tomorrow in the other? In 'Believe', I explore these questions through the intersections of culture, heritage, and identity. These poems reflect my own journey of embracing contradictions and finding strength in the spaces where past and present collide.

As an author, I see the world as a collection of interconnected stories—where the past shapes who we are, and the present leaves room for the futures we create. Writing 'Believe' has been my way of grappling with the question: Who am I when so many voices, histories, and stories shape me? My background is shaped by diverse influences, and these poems reflect the journey where legacies meet dreams.

But Believe is not just about me—it's about all of us. It's about how we are all shaped by the intersections of our pasts and the choices we make. We carry stories within us, often unnoticed, stories of ancestors whose voices shape our steps. At the same time, we continue writing our own stories of hope, growth, and transformation.

As you read Believe, I invite you to reflect on your own journey. These poems are a conversation between the past and the present, with moments of tension, longing, and reconciliation. I hope you'll find pieces of your own story here—moments of introspection, remembrance, and creation in the space between what has been and what is to come.

The beauty of this journey lies in embracing its complexity. In the mix of cultures, histories, and identities, there is strength. I hope *these poems remind you that we are all, in our own ways, a blend of many things—past and present, inherited and chosen—and that this complexity is where our true strength and beauty lie.*

Thank you for being part of this journey. May these words inspire you to reflect on your own intersections of history, identity, and dreams, and to see the beauty in the tangled, mixed threads that make you who you are.

Aarna Kapoor

11/26/2024

Acknowledgements

Every poem in Believe is a thread in the tapestry of my life, woven with love, history, and the voices of those who have shaped me. This book is as much theirs as it is mine.

To my parents, who taught me the value of roots and wings—thank you for instilling in me a deep respect for our heritage while encouraging me to explore and express my individuality. Your belief in me has been my greatest strength.

To my grandparents, the silent architects of our legacy, your stories, wisdom, and resilience echo through these pages. You are the bridge between past and present, and I am endlessly grateful for the paths you've paved.

To my sister, my confidence and partner in endless dreams—thank you for being my biggest cheerleader and for sharing in the laughter, the chaos, and the quiet moments that make life beautiful.

To the readers of this collection, you hold in your hands more than poetry; you hold fragments of my soul, reflections of the shared human experience, and a celebration of the intricate mosaic that is identity. Thank you for stepping into these words and letting them become part of your own story.

And finally, to the essence of what Believe represents—the harmony of cultures, the strength in diversity, and the beauty in belonging. May this book remind us all of the powerful intersections that define who we are.

ACKNOWLEDGEMENTS

With all my gratitude and love,
Aarna Kapoor
11/26/2024

Prologue

Who are you when the mirror reflects more than just your face?

When it whispers stories of ancestors you've never met, traditions you never asked for, and dreams you're still learning to claim?

Believe is not just a collection of poems—it's an excavation. Each word digs into the layers of identity: the familiar, the foreign, the forgotten. It questions the lines we draw between heritage and individuality, between the weight of our past and the lightness of our future.

This book was born out of conflict and reconciliation—the clashing of cultures, the dance of belonging, and the quiet rebellion of forging something new. It's for anyone who has ever felt torn between worlds or has stood at the crossroads of who they were taught to be and who they want to become.

But this isn't just my story. It's yours too, in ways you might not expect. These pages hold fragments of journeys like yours—filled with questions, contradictions, and moments of clarity that feel like home.

So, turn the page. Step into the unknown. Let's unravel these mixed threads together.

1. Fragment's Of break And Path For Self-Discovery

Love in life often feels like a powerful wave,
especially when someone close drifts away.
In those moments, we begin to question—
did they truly deserve our trust,
or were they just a like a feetling mirage?

When the truth dawns, it cuts deep,
leaving emotions teetering on the edge of chaos.
Yet, there's a quiet strength in the aftermath—
the choice to rise above the pain.

To reveal the best version of ourselves,
a side they never cared to see.
In doing so, the cracks in our hearts begin to heal,
and the weight of resentment slowly fades.

Love is a labyrinth—
intricate, tangled, and timeless.

*But in the end, aren't we all searching
for the trutest, bestest parts of who we are?*

2. Weight Of Faith To Prove

It takes just a moment to make mistakes,
Errors scatter on a path that shakes.
Two roads diverge, both seeming grand,
Tasks demand trust, a steady hand.

Dark phases test and prove us wrong,
Yet guide us to where we belong.
The right task waits just by your side,
Faith and trust become your guide.

Belief—just a word, fragile and small,
Until you prove it, and conquer it all.

3. Creator's Diminshing Skill :How Ai Redefines Itself

AI, like nature, in silence looks,
Ignored by us, yet writing new books.
Its depths unfold as we draw near,
With hidden parts and edges unclear.

Born of our minds, yet wild and free,
A shadow of human complexity.
As we lean on circuits, we slowly fade,
Our spark grows dim in the world we made.

Forgotten creators, hands turned cold,
While AI stands tall, both new and old.
Indifferent still, it hums along—
A quiet force, both weak and strong.

It leads us to see, we once were bold,
Our courage bright, like fires of gold.
But now remains the unyielding AI,

AARNA KAPOOR

Endless, while our own will runs dry.

4. Injustice Fades, Truth Prevails

The wonders of the world, famous and grand,
Told in the memories of great legends' hands.
History, which may once repeat itself,
With bright stars shining high, though not the brightest felt.

A world of fools, training once again,
For something great while striving for gain.
We saw things of equal importance rise,
But corruption lingers, hidden in disguise.

We tried to stop it, to bring it to an end,
But somewhere it still lurks, refusing to bend.
Our world won't be safe, not until we act,
To justify our actions, and face the facts.

Justice delayed is justice denied,
Let's not allow it to vanish or hide.
Let us act, let truth take its place,
And not let it fade in history's dark embrace.

5. Karma's Echoes Of Woods

In dark woods where shadows lie,
People taste the depths of hidden skies.
Truths buried deep, unseen, unknown,
Believed in silence, but never shown.

Whispers of secrets bind the town,
While some glimpse life's taste, ups and downs.
A city of trials, of journey's weight,
Where hardships bloom and twist to fate.

They say when souls pass, karma holds away,
Yet here, alive, belief finds its way.
For this city, steeped in mystery,
Unfolds the truth we're meant to see.

6. The Seizing Journey :Life

Life is often a trail, chasing success,
When it feels like a race, few will step back.
Even now, there's no time for those we love,
As we get caught in the competition within.

Life is a long journey, with moments of pain,
Like fighting a battle, enduring through strain.
But brighter days are always ahead,
And life, believe me, is full of beauty with faith ahead.

You have the charm to seize it all,
So just keep fighting, standing tall.
I know you'll emerge victorious and strong,
Earning the rewards you've worked for all along.
so don't worry as your charm is just about to shine
and brighten your charm and get ready to sparkel your life

7. Reflections of Truth and Failure

I used to be played, and I still get played.
I have two sides, like the world—one of truth, the other of
failure.
I help people learn and make their memories beautiful.
I only serve those who know how to handle me.

Sometimes, I show the good side, sometimes the bad,
And it all depends on the circumstances.
Even though I'm circular and can't walk,
When they use me, it makes me feel fulfilled.

It's God's creativity that made me this way,
And as a coin, I am proud of myself

8. Nature's Beauty

It was a thoughtful morning, with birds chirping,
And I was thrilled to see the sun in all its glory.
I felt a wave of energy flow through me,
So beautiful, it brightened my day, guiding me to follow the
sunshine.

As I ventured forward, it held me tight,
Showing me a line to hold on to.
But soon, I found myself lost in the middle of the woods.
For a moment, frustration took over,
Lost and uncertain—
Yet determined, I pressed on,
Until I finally found my way out of the maze of rays.

It made me furious, but also brought joy,
For when I found the path,
I realized that it was me all along—
I was the one to guide myself.

9. From Doubt to Triumph

It was full of challenges,
Filled with hard work.
At times, I wanted to quit,
But I still made my way to the end and won the race.

It pushed me to the edge,
Urging me to give up.
Somehow, it convinced me I might lose,
But lost in thought, something shifted.
A realization came, like flipping a coin,
And suddenly, everything changed.

My hard work became my path to victory,
And in the end, I made my family proud

10. The Journey Beyond Memories

Failure can't be fathomed,
As fading memories linger.
But determination is the key to success.
Where failure arises, there is always hope for a new ray.
The turning of light, or shall I say, a new chapter of life,
Rests on us.

When we fade those old memories, relief comes,
Yet a burning in our hearts remains.
Fading them away isn't the solution.
Now, winning is our goal—
Let's tear the failures of the past
And start anew,
Opening a new chapter of hope

11. Desire To Destiny

The pages of books, with ideas so pure,
They shape our thoughts, their wisdom endures.
Through life, they guide with gentle care,
Like leaves we turn, they're always there.

If a perfect friend you wish to find,
Books will always enrich your mind.
And when you're lost, just look within,
In books, you'll find your perfect kin.

Books empower, they make us whole,
With knowledge vast, they lift our soul.
To build a nation strong and bright,
They gift us strength, a guiding way to sucess.

Yet life, at times, seems so uncertain,
The deserving often left in despair.
While those who seek not, seem to gain,
But we press on, through joy and pain.

Though some may try to block our way,
To hide success, to lead astray,

BELIEVE

Life gives us tasks we must fulfill,
To carve our path, with iron will.

Life gives us tasks we must fulfill,
To carve our path, with iron will.

12. Seeking the Right Path in a Changing World

The world is full of success, where people hide their views,
Slowly turning towards the right path, finding their way
through.
What is this?
Successful people, once seeking the right path, now stand on the
edge,
Ready to fight for it.
What is this the world is showing us?
Is this the world we all desired,
Or is this just the beginning—or perhaps the end?

13. Beneath the Veil of Night

In the shadows of the dark, where lies are hidden somewhere,
Stories are kept as secrets, once cherished by all who care.
The world, like a coin, round and tossed,
Played with until its value was almost lost.
Is this all there is to know?

The stars in the sky, so bright and unique,
They guide us through nights, in silence they speak.
I gazed at many things, lost in thought,
Awake for days by the wonder they brought.

14. Through the Winds of Time

Sometimes, people make us feel worthless,
Yet, in the same breath, they show their own ignorance.
It's the way the world spins, and how we're treated.
Life is a marathon, relentless and unyielding,
Continuing until our final breath.

Time will ease our pain,
And turn moments of sorrow into joy.
So, embrace happiness,
For life is tough, and we are tougher.
In time, we'll see that the people who hurt us
Will change forever, never to be the same again.

15. Unfolding Life's Truths

As the new journey begins, the old memory fades,
We step forward, facing hurdles, yet a brighter path to sway.
The past, once heavy, we now let go,
For the future calls with a radiant glow.

Lost in yesterday, but today shines bright,
Life's uncertainties give way to newfound light.
When hope seems distant, slipping from views,
We rediscover hope in beginnings news.

We grow from what we were, into something more,
The past folds away as new truths we explore.
This journey, just started, is life's unfolding grace,
Where every step forward finds its better path.

16. Deep Wounds, Endless Time

In a world of fearful scars,
I wander through the remnants of past mistakes,
Once held tight, guarded with relentless care,
Yet now, they slip through time's grasp,
Like history passing, forgotten and forlorn.

People will forget,
That those scars were ever something real,
Deeply buried, hidden from the light,
Where mistakes once tightly bound descend,
Only to rise again,
When the same errors are repeated.

Is this the way the world works?
Can we alter this endless cycle,
Or are we bound to repeat it forevermore?

17. The Entrepreneur's Path

In the deep world of founders,
We found the chance to work, to grow,
To show our skills, as we dreamed,
Years of toil gave way to opportunity,
And we began to wonder at the paths we'd take.

From zero, we started,
And became heroes, at last,
Once laborers, now entrepreneurs,
Guided by the hands of fate,
Wondering at what we can achieve,
We realize, with faith,
We can hold the world in our hands.

18. Illumination Through Teaching

The beauty of teaching, a light so rare,
It shines through lives, with wisdom to share.
From minds unformed to souls that soar,
Teachers ignite dreams, and so much more.

They plant the seeds of thought and grace,
Guiding us forward, helping us trace
A path from ignorance to a life so bright,
Where we lead with courage, bathed in light.

Our knowledge, a garment of woven care,
A gift from teachers, beyond compare.
On this Teacher's Day, we bow and say,
Thank you for guiding us, lighting the way.

19. Guided By Light

It wasn't too late to start,
Nor too early to find the end,
A journey sparked by a flash of light,
A dream some chase, yet few transcend.

Not too far, nor too near,
It hovered within my reach,
But as I grasped, I woke in fear,
From stars that fearless, taught and preached.

They gathered round to lift me high,
To make me dynamic, bold, and true,
Yet I had to leave, with a sigh,
Guided by a light that grew.

A hope that led me to this place,
Where life's chapters intertwine,
To finish what I must embrace,
And claim this path as mine.

20. Pause and Reflect

Isn't it how people suffer,
Each day striving to fulfill their desires?
It makes me feel so grateful for the opportunity
To make our nation a place to live,
And a chance to join the race.

Our world is full of races—
Some run to fulfill their desires,
While others run to find more happiness.
But who in this world has the patience to sit and believe
That we could simply let the world be?

We all need to look back,
To see what we've achieved,
And realize we have time to enjoy this life.
We know life is limited,
Happiness is finite,
But the suffering to achieve it is long.

So let's sit down, relax,
And enjoy this small, fleeting life.

21. Secrets Unveiled in Success

When a spark of light shines bright,
Leading us through the tunnel,
Where success and secrets await,
And a state of trembling happiness resides.

People may wonder and begin to unveil
The secrets of achievement,
Where the mind finds satisfaction,
And hard work shapes our lives.

Where is the money?
Where the path seems right,
Yet the direction is a bit blurred,
We reach the place we all desired,

Receiving rewards of success,
And the sweet blossom of triumph
Guides our way,
Making our day
In the place we longed for

22. Beneath the Shining Skies

The true beauty of stars that shine,
Once carried scars and untold memories in their hearts.
Behind their glow lies a past, dark hidden,
A memory buried beneath layers of feeling and years.

They inspire many with their radiant light,
Yet keeping their pain concealed from sight.
We may not believe the scars they bear,
But at every step they take, we find inspiration.

Their unspoken brilliance brightens our days,
Letting us adore their beauty in every way.
They teach us to cherish each moment we have,
Guiding us gently toward our chosen path.

In their light, we too become stars,
Finding our own way, adoring who they were.

23. Maker's Way

It crafted a way of living,
And I chose the baker's path.
I woke each day to weave a tale,
One that had to journey far.

Along the way, money found its place,
But it made me wait, testing my patience.
So I sought the baker's secrets,
And in the journey, I uncovered an untold story.

It's the way the baker carved his life,
Busy every day, yet happy with what he achieved.
And that's how life goes on

24. The Burden of Desire

The desire to succeed lies within us,
Yet some days and nights are filled with pain,
When others make us question our destiny,
Taking our ideas and running with them,
It becomes a torment, making us rethink our trust
And our potential.
It's pointless to battle those who push us back,
Only to rise again and chase the dreams we once held with love.
We doubt ourselves, haunted by past mistakes,
And seek belief in a world of trustworthy souls,
Who might change the world.
But change cannot come
Until people admit their errors
And reshape this world into a better place to live.

25. Resilient Hearts

The fearless stares they gave us were no joke,

But it's truly hard to trust that person again.

It seems a small problem to everyone else,

But the one who faces it knows the real pain.

Yet that pain might lead to the destiny they desire.

Some think our hearts are made of stone,

That we are tough, unyielding.

But when you realize it's just a phase of life,

We turn to achieve our goals,

And not even the ones who doubted us,

Not family or friends who once pushed us down,

Can break us or pull us back.

Now, it's time to show the world who we are.

Author's Bio

Aarna Kapoor, aged 14 is a passionate secondary school student at Delhi Public School, currently in grade 9. With a strong interest in global affairs, Aarna Kapoor has participated in prestigious Model United Nations conferences such as SHISMUN, AYMUN, DPSIMUN, GD Goenka World MUN, and IITD MUN, earning appreciation and oral mentions. Outside academics, Aarna Kapoor is actively involved in sports, including gymnastics, skating, and yoga, and recently represented their school in the CBSE Yoga Cluster Competition '24. As an intern at Zenit Excelencia and a post-holder at the Sustainable Development Goals for Next Gen Council (WICCI), Aarna Kapoor is committed to making a positive impact on society. Aarna Kapoor also discovered a passion for writing poetry during Christmas, when they attended a writing workshop at Zenit Excelencia and learned to blend emotions into daily life.

Aarna Kapoor